SUPPLEMENT
to
Warwick County, Virginia
Colonial Court Records
in Transcription

Third Edition

Richard Dunn
Editor

CLEARFIELD

Printed for Clearfield Company by
Genealogical Publishing Company
Baltimore, Maryland
2016

ISBN 978-0-8063-5822-2

Made in the United States of America

Foreword

Researchers jump for joy when a long-lost county record comes to light—especially in a county like Warwick, where so many records have been lost through fire and war. And when records turn up a century and a half later (as did those that were taken from the Courthouse in 1865 and returned in 2012), we can hope that we might yet see something that was in a musty trunk in the attic.

Such wonderful finds are housed mainly by the Library of Virginia, and we are very grateful to LVA for its courtesy and helpfulness in presenting in full transcription these finds to other researchers. Our thanks go to Sandra Treadway and her staff and to John Metz for special help. Thanks also to Maria Sullivan for help with indexing.

A few little bits of info about this edition: Omissions are indicated by underlines (_) for part of a word or up to two words, and longer omissions (or omissions of unknown length) are indicated with the usual mark for ellipses (...). Torn pages and just illegible places are unfortunately common enough. Your editor's reading is by no means infallible, but effort has been made to be accurate throughout, all editorial emendations being within square brackets.

Shortening of words is done in the original manuscripts with a sign over the word. These signs are omitted here as those symbols are unavailable & seem unnecessary.

Spelling is sometimes automatically 'corrected' to modern usage (without the editor's control).

For simplifying use of the index the reader should consult the preceding page and the following page, as the item may extend over more than a single page.

The figures [Sr.] or [Jr] are inserted where a distinction of generations makes it seem necessary to avoid confusion.

Table of Contents

page

[1685 Petition of Thomas Ballard:]   To his Excellency Francis Lord Howard
Baron of Effingham his Maj[e]sties Lieutenant and Govern[or] Generall of Virginia
And to the Hon[ora]ble Councill of State **David [Crafford?]** by **Thomas Ballard** his
Attorney That your pet[ition] brought by Capt. Roger Jones 3 Indians viz A woman, a
boy and a Girl, who ran away from him in 3 or 4 dayes after had had bought them,
and made those ... to M[r] **Henry Batts** in Appomattox in Henrico County, who soon
after sold the boy to Mr **Peter [Proby?]** of Warwick County, from whom he also ran
away, and coming to your pet[itioner]s house, he ordered him to be [carried?] ... to
[Probys?], but finding by the [people?] of his family that he called severall of them
by their names, and had observable markes upon him, your pet[itioner] ... where
upon [Proby?] ... your pet[itioner] to Warwick Court the 22nd [day of] ... 1683, where
upon full ... the said Indian youth was adjudged to be your pet[itioner']s but in few
days he again Ran away and went to Mr **Henry Batts**, where he with the said
woman, his mother and his sister still remain as your pet[itioner] is informed, and
although your pet[itioner] hath ... advised him to return him ... he hath obstinately
refused to doe, therefore your pet[itioner] hath [arraigned?] him to this Hon[ora]ble
Court, And humbly prayes order against the said Batts for ... delivering of the said
Indians and also such damages as are given by [order?] of Assembly for entertaining
Runaway [servants?] of [such?] And your pet[itioner] shall ever pray

[1688 Order Book (September leaf & November page]   [These pages are badly
damaged and often completely illegible. This transcription represents the best
interpretation that could be managed, but is surely not without error].

_y^e 2 of ... to _ **Holmes** _ _ **Jno Davis** [?]dif. ... & regulated ... being fully heard: _ is
therefore ordered to ... paymrnt of ye Summe of one hundred fifty & five pounds of
Tobacco and cask ...

In the diff^{ce} between **Sam^{ll} Simmons** plt & **Thomas Evans** def^t It is ordered the said
Evans ... payments y^e sd Simmons on order the Summe of five [?] hundred pounds of
Tobacco _ cask according to specialty with costs at_ ex$^-$.
Ordered y^e sherff **Hunt** _**Thompson jun^r** 1

The suite depending between **Thomas Jenkins** & **Andrew Yorgan** deft y^e Same fully
heard & there aping foe Cause of acton: A nonsuite is granted, upon request of ...
actuall damages

George Green upon his pett^n is Exempted out of the publique and County levy

Joseph Beals [?] servant to m^r **John Arobe** [?] being brought to this Court for
running away, _ _ appearance at this Court that he shall _ run away for _ _ of 23

1

days   It is ordered that the sherr^{ff} take y^e said Servant into custody until he receive
_enty _ upon his bare back well laid on

The diff^{ce} this Co^{rt} depending on a referf^{ce} from y^e last Court between m^r **Eman^{ll}
Wills** ... deft is againe referrd to y^e next Court

Ord^d y^t y^e Shrff Hunt ass$^-$of **Gyllain** _ Henry Thompson jun^r

Idem... idem upon his own acc^t

Upon y^e pet^n of m^r Wills in behalf of y^e orphants of **J^{no} Wills** Th- m^r **Andrew Cole** & -
exor (vide pet^n) _ upon y^e motion of m^r **Hugh Owen** att^{ny} of m^r Cole referred to y^e
next Court, at w^h time m^r Cole is to appeare

Whereas **George Robinson** hath in his custody belonging to ye orphant of one maire
and one cow and calf: and ye orphan being near at age & m^r **Behethland Crew** re[
]_ing that ye sd orphan may have ye same in _ possession: It is by ye Court granted,
the said m^r Crew obliegeng himself to save the Court harmless

Upon the pet^n of **Mary Muschamp**: It is ordered that the she bee possessed with her
decd husband's Estate, she having _ by ye oaths of m^r Jo_ _ & m^r Tho: Hopkins that it
was her sd husband... she paying all ... to same ... doeing whereof m^r John Chandler
became security ... harmless, _ is farther ordered that **Wm Bolton** __ bond
accor[dingly]

The Co^{rt} is adjord till ye 21th [sic] of 7 [September] next

At a court] held for Warwick ... of September – 1688   Psnt Maj^r **Harwood Capt
Whitaker Capt L_ Cary** m^r **Sam^{ll} Ransha_** m^r **Robert Hubbard**   m^r **William Cary**

Upon y^e pet^n of m^r **Thomas Phipps** in right of his wife (vide pet^n) ... estate of m^r _ a
L$^-$of Adm^r is granted unto y^e s^d Phipps he putting in Security for y^e Same according
to act – m^r **Anthony Haynes** & m^r **Eman^{ll} Wills** in open Co^{rt} have enterd themselves
Securities for s^d Adm^r

The diff^{ce} between **Jno Noble** plt & _ **Edward Loftis** deft is referred to [the next]
Court

A Nonsuite is grted to **Jeremiah Pierce** _ m^r **Andrew Cole** ... ye diff^{ce} between y^e -s^d
Cole & him ... s^d **Wm Cole** ... declaration according to law _ usuall Damages

m^r Andrew Cole & **Jno Lenton** for appeale _ m^r Wills & _ **Dodman** for m^r Dodman

2

m^r **Anthony Haynes** & m^r **Richd Moore** Security for m^r Wills

Adm^r grtd m^r **Andrew Lawrance** on ye Estate of his decd father m^r **Tho Lawrence** – Security **Jno Lenton** & **Ben Brock**

It is ordered y^t _ Estate of m^r _ **Lawrance** bee by **Matthew Jones, Behethland** & **Wm Ellinsworth** or any two of them bee appraysed between this & ye next court they being first sworn before a magistrate

Adm^r grtd **Isabella James** on her Husbands Estate Security **m^r Anthony Haynes** & **m^r Emanuel Wills**

Ordered t^t ye Estate of **Francis Janes** [Jones?] decd bee between this & y^e next Court appraised by m^r **Roger Daniell** m^r **James Pawly** & **Edward Rousorne** or any two of them they [being] first sworne before a magistrate

... & ... all time allowed m^r **Arobe**

m^r E_ ... surviving Son _of m^r **Dodman** by his A_nging his ... Dodman by virtue of a Certaine writeing unto his hand ... day of April 1672 & after marriage acknowledged in open co^{rt} ...

... shall accordingly ... that_ by him ... according to agrem^t _

The attachm^t grtd **m^r Thomas** as intermarryeing m^{rs} Thomas ag^t Ma_ Negro _ this Court renewed

It is ordered that **John Tingnall** _ as attorney of m^r **Richard Harris** _ out of the Estate of **Margarett Hatton** decd ye judgment of 400^{lbs} of Tob ... due by _: he haveing made ... sath y^t he never rec^d any satisfaction for ye same with ...

Whereas **Martha Greene** decd died intestate & left three small children and a very mean Estate, & **George Robinson** haveing married the sister of y^r sd Martha praying this Court for administration on the same wch ye Court conceives is not ... to be ... therefore order that the sd George Robinson be intrusted therewith ... & **Henry Whitaker** ... and farther ... sd Estate ... valued & appraised by ... John _ & **Mathew Wood** or any lawfully ... first sworne before a Majest_

Adm^n grtd Maj^r Harwood on the Estate of _ **Martha Moore** decd: Capt **Whitaker** & m^r **Hubberd** security

3

It is ordered Maj^r **Humphrey Harwood** be paid out of the Estate of m^s Martha Moore ye summe of 125 [lbs] of Tobacco & Cask ... ye same appearing due for ... And ... for raiseing [?] a young child ... for _ children _

Ordered that **Christanna Jardin** widow be intrusted wth Estate of her decd _ James Jardin who died intestate _ ye Estate being very small Conceives not also to be _ are ... be between the two of _ _they ... before ye next Majestrate... at the next Court

Will and _ on both Negroes belonging to Cold Cole being this day brought to Court to be adjudged or theire ages, are accordingly adjudged eight yeares of age

It is ordered that the Estate of **Margarett Hutton** _, be inventoried & appraised between _ & ye next Court by **John _oore, Darby Daniell** & **John Stow** or any two of them they being first sworn before ... Majestrates, & y^t **John Hatton** ... Exhibitt ye same

The Co^rt adjo^rd till ye xxi^th of 7^br next   from thence to y 10th of 9 [November] next

[1688 Order Book (page from November):] At a Court held for ...
10th day of Nov 1688   The House [?] ... Cole _
Psent   Maj. **Hump: Harwood**   _ **Merry**
Capt **Richard Whitaker**   m^r Em [?] **Wills**   **Miles Cary**   m^r **Sam^ll Ransha**   m^r **Robert Huberd**

Judm^t confest by **Will Gigges** for __ of five [?] hundred fifty pounds of Tob & cask __ And to m^r **And: Cole** ...

Judgmt confest ye sd Gigges for y payment of 12 _ being for _ Bill of E ... damage to m **H Harwood** ... with Costs of ...

A former order of this Court dated J 22^⁻[?] 1687 granted m^r _ **Wilson** for tenn pounds Six Sh: nine pence, long due _ _ Bills of ...75 _ ... agst m^rs _ **Martha Moore** [?] Adm [?] of her husband **R Moore** decd ... in the Court confirmed & ordered y^t Maj^r Harwood intrusted wth y sd Moore, _ pay him 12-0-3 act of y sd Moore ...

Ordered y^t **H Harwood** trustee of the estate of m^r Moore decd pay out of the sd Moor Estate to m^r **Sam^ll junr** 30 ...costs of suit _ _

Ordered y^t H Harwood trustee of the Estate of m^r Moor dect pay out of y sd Estate to m^r _ _ eight hundred pounds of _ & Cask & three pounds wth costs of suit [?] _

Ordered y^t H: Harwood trustee of y estate of m^r Moore ... pay out of y sd Estate to the Hon^bl **Nath Ballen**, ... wth costs

4

===
[1688 Judgment & Order, Giggs to Harwood:] Warw^k County At a co^{rt} held for the said County the 9^{br} [November] y^e 10th 1688

Prsent   His Maj^{ties} Justices of y^e Peace

Judgm" Confest by **Wm Giggs** to Maj^r **Humphrey Harwood** truste of the Estate of Mrs **Martha Moore** decd for y^e paym^t of twelve pounds & three pence sterll: being due on prtested [?] Bills of Exchange wth fifteen p[ounds] of damages   It is therefore ordered y^t he make paym^t of ye same to ye sd Harwood wth costs of suit als ex^n

A true copy   Test   **Miles Cary** C. Cur

Sherff {_ & bond   _

Clerk { ... on judgm^t & _} 5

{bill costs   3

63

[1689 Writ to sheriff re Wm Giggs]   The Content of ye wthin Judgm^t not being satisfied: These are in their Maj^{ties} Names to will & requir you to arrest ye body of ye wthin named Wm Giggs & him In safe Costody Detain without Bail _ _ bill ye wthin judgm^t wth costs be fully satisfied & paid to y^e sd Harwood hereof you are not to faile as alsoe to make due return of this writ dated this 28th day of Octo^{br} 1689

A true copy   test **Miles Cary** Cl

To y^e Sherff of War^k County or his Deputy

here on other Side		63 }
Execun & record	35 }	98
Sheriff _		100
		198

Ex$^-$ ... Mag^r Hump Harwood _ _ **Wm Hubbard** Sub Sherf ...

[1689 Wills v Lisny, capias:] Warw^k County ss   These are in their Maj^{ties} names to will & require you to arrest y^e body of Mr **Emanuel Wills** & him in safe Costody detain till he Enter into bond wth sufficient sureties for his appearance before their Maj^{ties} Justices of ye Peace at ye next Court held for this County to answer ye suit of **Ralph Lisny** in an action of ye case hereof you are not to faile as alsoe to make due returne of this writ dated this 15th day of July 1689

To ye Sheriff of Warw^k County or his deputy   **Miles Cary** Cl Cur

[reverse:] July ye 16th 1689 Executed __ **Robt Hubberd**

[at 90 degrees:] Capias Wills vs Lisny

[1707 complaint, Bates v Loftis:]   Warwick County ss   May Court anno Domini 1707   **James Bates** complaines against Edward Loftys of this County of a plea upon the case for that to witt that: Whereas the foresd Edward Loftis standeth justly indebted to the said James Bates of Yorke County in the sum of two poundes & five shillings in good current payable money as by his certain writeing under his hand: dated the third day of September in the year of our Lord God one thousand seaven hundred & six which the sd James brings here in Court dated as aforsd & signed by

5

the sd Edward wherein the sd Edward doth promise & oblidge himself his heirs – to pay to the sd James Bates on Ord⁻the sum of Twenty [pounds] & five shillings in good current payable money after the thirty first of January [?] then next following the date of the sd noate or writeing notwithstanding the said Edward Loftys his said promise of asssumpsitt __ regarding but fraudulently continueing the __ on his part craftily & subtilly to deceive & do fraud: the foresaid sum of two: poundes & five shillings in money as aforesd: Although often demanded by the sd Jamess yet the said Edward to him hath not payd nor any part thereof but the same to pay or render to the sd James hath hitherto denyed and still refuseth therefore he saith he iss damnified & hat damage to the value of four poundes sterll: & thereof he brings suite _

[1715 Release, Naylor to Goldestone:] This indenture made the eighth day of October in the year of our Lord Christ one thousand seven hundred and fifteen between **Joshua Naylor** of Denbigh Parish in the County of Warwick ... Planter of the one part and **William Goldestone** of the County of Gloucester ship-carpenter of the other part Witnesseth that I the said Joshua Naylor for and in consideration of the sume of thirty pounds current money of Virginia to him in hand paid by the said William Goldestone on or before the ensealing and delivery hereof the receipt of whereof the said Joshua Naylor doth hereby acknowledge and thererof and every part and parcel thereof doth acquit and discharge the said William Goldestone his heirs executors and administrators and every of them by these presents hath given granted aliened released and confirmed and by these presents doth give grant alien release and confirme unto the said William Goldestone and unto his heirs and assignes all that pla[n]tation seat or dividend of land scituate leying and being in the Parish of Denbigh and County of Warwick aforesaid on the East side of Deep Creek and running from thence east one hundred and two polls to a pine, thence south east eighty six degrees one hundred and thirty two polls to a pine thence to a line of old marked trees eighty polls to a corner gum tree standing by the Loane Pond thence south west sixteen degrees fifty polls to a white oak corner tree thence north, eighty six degrees west to two sap [ling?] pines standing on the east side of the pine tree gut thence down the said gut to the beginning place the same being part of a patent of three hundred to me granted to **Richard Dixon** dated the seventeenth day of January one thousand six hundred and sixty five and by the last Will and Testament of the said Richard Dixon devised unto him the said Joshua Naylor and his heirs for ever containing ninety six acres together with all houses outhouses edifices buildings yards gardens orchards woods underwoods, timber trees ways waters ... profits commodities hereditaments and appurtenances whatsoever the same premises or any part thereof belonging or in any wise appertaining all which said premises now are in the actuall possession of the said William Goldestone by virtue of one indenture of bargain and sale to him thereof made for the term of one year bearing date the day before the date of these

6

presents and made between the said Joshua Naylor of the one part and the said William Goldestone of the other part and by virtue of the statute for transferring _ into possession and all the estate right title interest use trust property ... claim and demand whatsoever of the said Joshua Naylor of in and to ... said premises and every or any part and parcel thereof and the reversion or reversions remainder or remainders yearly and other rents and pro_ ... premises and every part and parcel thereof and ... writeings records scripts and muniments what_ ... concerning the said premises or any part thereof ... seat or dividend of land ... _gular other the premises herein before mentioned meant or intended to be_ given granted aliened released and confirmed ... concerning the said premises and every pa_ ... thereof with their and every of their appurtenances unto the said **William Goldestone** his heirs and assignes to the only proper use and behoofe of him the said William Goldestone his heirs and assigns for ever to be held of our Sovereign Lord the King his heirs and successors by the rents and services therefore due and of right accustomed to be paid for the same and the said Joshua Naylor for his heirs and assigns the said mentioned granted premises with the appurtenances and every part and parcel thereof unto the said William Goldestone his heirs and assignes against the said Joshua Naylor or any other person or persons whatsoever shall and will warrant and for ever defend _ these presents and the said Joshua Naylor for his heirs executors and administrators and for every of them doth hereby covenant grant and agree to and with the said William Goldestone his heirs and assignes and to and with every of them by these presents in manner and form following (that is to say) that he the said Joshua Naylor now is and standeth lawfully rightfully and absolutely seized of the said plantation seat or dividend of land and all and singular other the premises herein before meant mentioned _ intended to be hereby given granted aliened released confirmed and every part and parcel with their and every of their appur[tenances] of a good sure perfect and inde_ estate of inheritance in fee simple And that at the time of the ensealing and delivery thereof full power right and Lawfull and absolute authority to grant and convey the same unto the said William Goldestone his heirs and assignes for ever in manner and form aforesaid and that he the said William Goldestone his heirs and assignes shall and will from time to time and at all times hereafter peaceably and quietly enter into and upon have hold occupy possess and enjoy _ his and their proper use and behoofe the aforesaid premises with all and singular the appurtenances herein before mentioned Without any lawfull or equitable _ suit trouble denyall disturbance expulsion interruption claim and dem[and] of the said Joshua Naylor or any other person or persons whatsoever claiming or to claim any estate right title or interest of in or out of the said premises or any part thereof and that free and clear and freely and clearly exonerated _ and discharged or otherwise upon request thereof to be made well and sufficiently saved harmless and indemnified by the said Joshua Naylor his heirs executors administrator of and from all Manner of former and other _ gifts grants bargaines sales feoffments Leases estates mortgages ... fees fines forfeitures

7

judgments extents executions rents and arrears of rents and of and from all manner of former and ... charges and incumbrances whatsoever had made caused omitted comitted done or suffered or to be had made caused omitted comitted ... by the said Joshua Naylor his heirs or assignes or by any of them _ by any other person or persons whatsoever and lastly that he the ... his heirs and assignes shall and will from time to time and at all times hereafter dureing the space of seven years next ensuing ... at the reasonable request and costs and charges in the law of the said William Goldestone his heirs and assignes or any of them make doe acknowledge Levy execute and suffer or cause to be made done acknowledged leveyed executed and suffered all and every such further and other lawful and reasonable act and acts thing and things device and devices conveyances and assureances in the law whatsoever for the better and more perfect and absolute conveying and assureing the said premises with their and every of their appurtenances unto the said William Goldestone his heirs and assignes as by him the said William Goldestone his heirs and assignes or his or their council learned in the law shall be reasonably devised advised or required   In Witness hereof the said Joshua Naylor hath hereunto sett his hand and seale the day and year above written.   Joshua Naylor [torn]

Sealed and Delivered in the presence of us Miles Cary **William Young** his mark Richard Cary   At a Court held for Warwick County on Thursday y^e _ of December _   This release was presented in Court by William Goldestone at whose request the same was presented by the oath of Miles Cary Richard Cary two of the witnesses thereto and is at the request of the said Wm Goldestone admitted to record.   Test Miles Cary C Cur_   And at the same Court **Elizabeth Naylor** relict of the wi_ Joshua Naylor deced came in to Court & being first privately examined directs relinquished all her right of dower of in and to the within mentioned land & premises unto the within named William Goldestone and is recorded in the County Records   test   Miles Cary C Cur_

[1716, Will of Henry Cary :]   In the Name of God Amen I **Henry Cary** of the County of Warwick being Sick in body but of Sound and perfect mind and memory Praise be given to Almighty God for the Same, do make and Ordain this my last Will and Testament in manner and form following, and first I commend my Soul into the hands of Almighty God beseeching him to grant me Full remission and pardon for all my Sins by the Merits and for the Sa_ of my most Blessed and Redeemer Christ Jesus and by whom I hope to inherit a Joyful Resurection, and as for that worldy Estate which it hath pleased God to bestow upon me, I give and bequeath the Same in manner and form following hereby revoking and making void all former Wills by me heretofore made and Declaring this Will to be my Last Will & Testament   I Will and Ordain that all my Just Debts and funeral Charges be paid and Discharged by my Executor hereafter named and after my Debts of _ are So paid and Discharged as aforesd my Will and desire is that all the Remainder of my personal Estate of what Kinds Soever as Negroes Stock household Goods money Tobacco or any things Else

8

be equally divided between my Son **Henry Cary** _ Cary my daughter **Anne Stuckey** my daughter **Elizabeth Casbrook** and my late Daughter **Judith Barbers** [sp?[two Sons **Thomas Barber & William Barber** Except my Negro Girl Named Rachel who I give and bequeath to my Son Henry Cary & his heirs forever.

And lastly I do hereby Nominate and appoint my Said Son Henry Cary whole & sole Executor of this my last Will and Testament In Witness whereof I have hereunto _ my hand & Seal this 27th day of January 1716   Henry Cary   [seal]   Signed Sealed Published & Declared in the presence of **Rob**t **Philipson Miles Cary**   [and **Richard Cary**]   At a Court held for Warwick County on Thursday the first of September 1720 [?] This will was presented in Court by Henry Cary junr the Executor who made Oath thereto and being proved bychat is better the Oaths of **Miles Cary** and **Richard Cary** two of the Witnesses thereto is admitted to record. And is recorded in the County records. Teste Richard Cary C Cur_

   [on reverse:] The Last Will & Test_ of Mr. Henry Cary

[1717, Will of Albridgton Jones:]   In the name of God amen I Albridgton Jones of Warwick County bring Sick and weak in body but in perfect sense [?] and memory thanks be to God for it – constitute [?] and appoint this my last will and testament in manner and form following—Item I give and bequeath my soul unto the hands of Almighty God my body to the Earth to have Christian buriall in sure and sertain hope of [joy]full resurection at the last day   Item my [will and] disire is that all my ... debts ... be first payd   Item   My will and disire is that ... divided between my loving wife **Elizabeth Jones** and my three daughters **Elizabeth Jones** [jr], **Martha Jones** and **Agatha Jones** and in case that either of my three daughters should die in there minority or without heirs lawfully begotten that th[eir] part to goe to the survivors ...   Item   My will and desire is that my loving wife have the use of my whole estate both real and personall during her widowhood and that the Estate be not inventoryed till her marage or death and my will and desire is that Mr. **John [W]ills** and my loving wife **Elizabeth Jones** be my whole and Sole ... and Execut[ors of] this my last will and testament Witnesseth my hand this 10th february ... [1717] Alb: Jones sealed   Signed and sealed ...In the
                   presence of us **Cuthbert Hubbard Michael Cox**
   At a court held for Warwick County on Thursday the fifth of June 1718 This will was presented in court by Elizabeth Jones one of the Executors who made oath ... and being provd by the oaths of Cuthbert Hubbard and Michael Cox the witnesses thereto is admitted to record.   [The following items (on the reverse side of the foregoing) evidently are related to other actions.]   In open [court] ... Thomas Haynes [seal] Robt Philipson [seal]   Richard Cary 1718

   At a Court held for Warwick County of Thursday the fifth of June 1718 The wit[hin] named ... [torn] [**Thomas H]aynes** and **Robert Philipson** Gentlemen came into Court and acknowledged __ to be their proper Pet. [Petition?] and deed to _

9

Sovereign Lord the King his heirs and Successors. Whereupon it is Committed to record.

Warwick County _ Wee the Subscribers do declare, that we do believe that there is not any Transubstantiation in the Sacrament of the Lords Supper or in the Ellements of bread and wine at or before the consecration thereof by any person whatsoever. Given under our hands this 9th day of June 1718   **Nath: Hoggard   Enos Mackintosh**

[171_Selden's complaint v John Lucas and 1718 judgment:] Samuel Selden complains of John Lucas in a plea that to wit that whn he the said John the tenth Day of November in the year of our Lord 1716 was indebted unto the said Samuel in the sum of fifty shillings current money for certain services by him at the special instance & request of him the said ... for him before that time done & the formed to wit for appearing & argueing for him as his attorney in the General Court of this Colony and being so jedged afterward to wit the same day & year aforesaid at Denby in this County aforesaid on himself did assume & to the sd Samuel then & there did faithfully promise to pay him the same whn he should be thereunto requested yet he the said John his promise & assumption little regarding the sd fifty shillings to the said Samuel tho often thereto requested hath not paid by the same to pay hath hitherto & still doth gainsay to the plts damage _ pounds current money & thereof he brings suit

Samuel Selden in pria persona

[reverse:] Samuel Selden ag **John Lucas** Case 5 Current money dam March Court 1718 Order against the Sherriff Test **M Cary** CCur April Court 1719 Judgm granted The ptr for 25/ and costs   Test M Cary C cur

[1718 Writ to Sheriff to arrest John Lucas:] Warwick County ss These are in his Majesty's Name to wil and require you to arrest the body of John Lucas and him in your safe custody to keep til he enter into bond with sufficient security for his appearance before his Majesty's Justices of the Peace at the next court to be held for this County then and there to answer the suit of Samuel Selden in an action upon the case of Damage five pounds current money herein you are not to fail also make due return hereof dated this 23rd day of January 1718

[March 1718, Selden v Hoggard] At a Court held for Warwick County on Thursday y[e] 5th of March 1718
Judgment being this Day past unto Samuell Selden against **Nathaniell Hoggard** Gent: Sheriff of this County for the Sum of five pounds Current money and Costs by reason of the non appearance of John Lucas in an action upon the Case at the Suit of the Said Samuell Selden on the motion of the said Nathaniell Hoggard an attachment is

Granted him against the Estate of the Said John Lucas for the aforesaid Sum and costs returnable to the next Court for Judgment   Copy test Miles Cary
   [reverse panel:] Attachm^t Hoggard _ Lucas

[1718 Writ to Sheriff, John Lucas, attachment:]   Pursuant to the within order   Warwick County ss   These are in his Majesty's name to will and require you to attach Soe much of the Estate of the within named John Lucas as shall be of value sufficient to satisfy and pay the within judgment and costs and the Same to secure_ to provide that it may be forthcoming at the next Court for further proceedings thereon to be had. Herein you are not to faile as also make due return thereof dated this 9th Day of March 1718   To the Sherriff of Warwick County or his Deputy Miles Cary C. Cur: March ye 26th 1719 Executed on a negrow wooman named Combo

[1719 Bond of Mary Crew et al] Know all men by these presents that wee **Mary Crew Henry Cary** and **John Whitaker** all of Warwick County are held and firmly bound unto the worshipfull his Majesty's Justices of the Peace for the said County of Warwick in the full and just Sum of Fifty pounds of lawfull money of great Britain to which payment well and truly to be made to the said Justices their heirs Executors and Administrators jointly and Severally firmly by these presents In witness whereof we have hereunto sett our hands and Seals this Second Day of Aprill anno_ Domini 1719
          The Condition of this Obligation is such that if the above bound Mary Crew Administratrix of all the Goods Chattels and Creditts of **Ralph Battran** decd do make or cause to be made a true and perfect inventory of all and singular the goods chattels and creditts of the said Decd which have or shall come to the hands possession or knowledge of her the said Mary crew or into the hands or possession of any other person or persons for her and the Same so made do Exhibite or cause to be Exhibited into the County Court of Warwick at such time as she shall be thereto required by the said Court and the same goods chattels and credits and all other the goods chattel and credits of the said decd at the time of his death which at any time after shall come to the hands of possession of the said Mary Crew or into the hands and possession of any other person or person for her Do well and truly administer according to law and further do make a just and true account of her actings and doeings therein when thereto required by the said Court, and all the rest and residue of the said goods chattels and credits shall be found remaining upon the said Administratrix account the same being first examined and allowed by the Justices of the Court for the time being shall deliver and pay unto such person or persons respectively as the said Justices by their order or judgment shall direct pursuant to the laws in that _ made and provided, and if it shall hereafter appear that and last Will and Testament was made by the said decd and the Executor or Executors therein named do exhibite the same in the said Court making request to

11

have it allowd and approved accordingly if the said Mary Crew being thereunto
required do render and deliver up her Letters of Administration approbation of such
Testament being first had and made in the said Court the this obligation to be void
and of none effect otherwise to remain in full force and Virtue.
Mary Crew [seal]

    Sealed and Delivered in open Court   **Henry Cary** [seal]
                                         John Whitaker [seal]

[1725 Will of Thomas Mallicote:]   In the name of God Amen   I Thomas Mallicote
being very sick in body but in perfect sense of memory praised be Almighty God, do
make this my last Will & Testament in manner & form as followeth Imp^s I give &
bequeath my soule into the hands of Allmighty God my maker hoping through the
merits of Jesus Christ my Saviour to live with him at the last day to eternall bliss &
glory and my body to the Earth from whence it was taken to be buried in Christian
Buriall according to the discretion of my executor hereafter named as for my
temporal estate as followith   Item I give & bequeath unto my wife **Mary Mallicote**
[sr] a negro boy my great Bible Family Prayer Book great black walnut table & on
gray colte the I bought of John Wheeler forever Item   I give & bequeath unto my
son **John Mallicote** Quashey a negro man the least [last?] of my black walnut tables
& & the whole duty of man forever. Item I give & bequeath unto my daughter
Frances Mallicote Judy a negro girle & the Practis of Piety forever.   Item   I give
and bequeath unto my daughter Mary Mallicote Dianer a negro girle forever I I
give & bequeath unto my son **Thomas Mallicote [jr]** the child that my negro woman
Betty now goes with if it do well if not the first that does live Tomboy a negro man
and ten pounds current forever   Item I give & bequeath unto my loving wife **Mary
Mallicote** my- mare forever It is my will & desire that my loving wife shou'd have
the work of my sons negroes till they come of age and if it should please God that
either of my children shoud doe without heir of the body lawfully begotten then my
will & desire is that my loving wife should layout two hogg^s of Tob^o for the family's
use and that the remainder be sold for mony and all the rest of my worldly estate
and goods which God hath indowed me with all my debts and funeral expences
being first paid I give unto my loving wife three sons & two daughters to be equally
divided amongst them and of this my last Will & Testament I doe make and ordaine
my loving wife Mary Mallicote to whole & sole executrix as Witness my hand & seal
_ fifth day of Decem^r 1725   Whereas a negro woman named Betty has not been
mentioned I give the said negro to my loving wife during her life & after her deced
the said negro & her increase to be equally divided among my above ment^d children
Thos Mallicote [seal]

    Signed sealed and acknowledged in presence of us **Wm Bressie John Edwards**
John _   At a court held for Warwick County of Thursday the _ day of Augt 1726
This will (& codicil) was presented in Court by Mary Mallicote the ext^x therein
named who made oath thereto according to law & bein proved by the oaths of

Willim Bressie John Edwards & **John Le_** the witness thereto they were admitted to record Test R. Gough C.C.

A Copy Teste Richd Cary C.C.   [reverse:] a copy of Thomas Mallicotes Will

1727 Phillipson v Hyde] ... Warwick County ... May Court MD... **Robert Phillipson** Gent and **Dorothy Peare** widow complain ags **Richard Hyde** in Custody & of a plea upon the case for that _ he the said deft the 5th day of June MDCCXXVii At the parish of Warwick in the County aforesaid was indebted to the Plts in the Sum of fifty five Shillings Cur^t mony ... for diverse goods by the said Plts to the said deft then & there sold and delivered and the said Deft being so indebted as aforesaid by his certain writing obligation _ bearing date the same day and year at the parish afores^d in the County aforesaid upon himself did assume and to the said Plt did then & there faithlfully promise that he would pay the said fifty five shillings to the ... by the last day of December then next following, Nevertheless the said _ his promise and assumption aforesd in form aforesaid was ... regarding, but de_ and fraudulently intending them the said Plt in this behalf craftily and subtilly to deceive and defraud the said fifty five shillings to the said plts or either of them altho' often required to wit the twenty fifth day of April in the year of our Lord MDCXXVii hath not paid but the same to them to pay hath he ... together
[fragment ends]

[1729 William Cole's will]   In the name of God amen I **William Cole [sr]** of the County of Warwick Gent being very sick and weak in Body but of perfect memory and understanding Do make this my last will and Testament in form and manner following Imprimis I give and bequeath my mortal soul unto the hands of Almighty God my heavenly Father hoping for redemption of all my sins through the merits of Jesus Christ my Saviour and my body to the Earth to be decently intered at the discretion of my Executors herein named. And as for my worldly Estate, wherewith it hath pleased God to bless us, after my Just debts and funeral expenses are paid I dispose of the same as followeth I give and devise all my Lands lying and being in the County of Goochland to my three Sons **John Cole, Roscow Cole**, and **James Cole** and their Heirs for ever to be equally divided between them. Item I give and bequeath to my loving wife **Mary Cole** for ever two Negroes named Will and Sarah above and besides her Dower in my lands and Negroes as also one ninth Part of my Personal Estate. Item I give and bequeath to my loving Son **William Cole [jr]** for ever one Negro boy named Lewis, and whereas my late Brother **James Roscow** Esqr by his last will bequeathed to my Son, John Cole one hundred Pounds to be paid out in Negroes for the use of the said John Cole which hundred Pounds I have received of the Executor of the said **James Roscow** and have appropriated two Negro boys named Gaby and Bob and two Negro Girls named Moll and Betty for that use I do hereby give and bequeath to my said Son John Cole for ever the said Negroes Gaby, Bob, Moll, and Betty, in lieu of the said hundred pounds. Item All the rest and

13

residue of my Negroes and Personal Estate of what kind or Nature So ever, I give and bequeath, to my Children **William Cole,** John Cole, Roscow Cole, James Cole, **Mary Cole [jr],** **Jane Cole** & **Susannah Cole,** for ever to be equally divided among them the Survivors or Survivor Share and Share alike. My Will also is and I do hereby order that my Executors do work all my Negroes (except those particularly bequeathed) on my Lands at their discretion until my son William arrive to the age of twenty one years and the profits of the said Lands and Negroes to be equally divided among all my Children as aforesaid and in case my son William __ Sue for or demand account of my said Executors from or for using or working the intailed Lands that then and in such case I give and bequeath all the residue of my said Negroes and personal Estate to my Children **John Cole, Roscow Cole, James Cole, Mary Cole, Martha Cole, Jane Cole,** and **Susannah Cole** My Will also is and I do hereby constitute and appoint my loving friends **Cole Diggs** Esqr, **Lewis Burnwall** Gent. And my loving wife **Mary Cole [Sr.]** (to whom I also give and devise the Guardianship and Tuition of all my Children) Executors of this my last will and Testament and my loving friend **William Roscow Gent.** to be trustee thereof hereby revoking and annulling al former or other Wills and testaments by me made In Witness whereof I have hereunto set my hand and Seal this first day of November in the third year of the Reign of our now Sovereign Lord George the Second and in the year of our Lord one thousand Seven hundred and Twenty nine

And in case my loving wife **Mary Cole** [sr] should be now with Child and such Child should be born alive then I give and bequeath to such Child an equal Part with the others of my Personal Estate and Negroes.   Wm Cole [seal]

   Signed Sealed Published and delivered to _ his last Will and testament by the said **William Cole** and the Witnesses under written. Subscribed their names in the presence of the said testator (the word) (Lands and) between the fifteenth and Sixteenth lines [the 14th & 15th lines are probably meant; here the numbers would be 10 & 11] the words (for ever between the Sixteenth & Seventeenth lines the word (Survivors or Survivor) between the twenty ninth and thirtieth lines [here 19 & 20] the word (the word 'account') between the thirty fourth and thirty Sixth [sic] lines and the _ twenty Sixth line first interlined and made. **William Roscow, William Hopkins, James Padin.**

   Virginia _   At a General Court held at the Capitol November the first MDCCXXIX This Will was presented in Court by **Lewis Burnwell** Gentleman one of the Executors therein named who made oath to it according to Law and William Roscow and **James Rodin** two of the Witnesses to it made oath that on the first day of October last they saw the said William Cole sign Seal and Publish it as his Will and that he was then in perfect sense & memory whereupon the said will was admitted to record.

Teste R. Hickman CGC   A Copy Teste John Brown CGC

14

[1750 Will of Nathaniel Wythe:]   In the Name of God Amen   I **Nathaniel Wythe** of the parish & County of Warwick gent being sick & weak of body but of Disposing Mind & Memory do make & ordain

This my last Will & Testament in manner following   I comend my Soul to God that gave it & my body to the earth to be decently buried at the Discretion of my Exor hereafter named And as to that worldly Estate I am blessed with I give & dispose hereof as followeth   Item I give & bequeath unto my loving wife **Eliz^a Wythe** all my Slaves that I am possessed not entailed [?] with to her & her Disposal and all my personal Estate   Item I give unto my said Wife my Land in Prince George County during the Term of her natural life. And after her death I give the said land in Prince George County to that child my wife is now with child with & to its heirs forever Lastly I appoint my friends **Beverley Whiting** & **Thomas Todd** of Gloucester County gent and my wife Eliz^a Wyth Exors of this my last Will & Testament hereby revoking all former or other wills by me at any time heretofor made Declaring _this only to be my last Will & Testament In Witness whereof I have hereunto set my hand & seal the twenty Sixth Day of Feby 1750

   Signed Sealed published & declard by the Tes'or to be his last Will & Testament In presence of   [blank or torn off] [seal]

   At a Court held for Warwick County August 1st 1751   This writing was presented in Court as the last Will & Testament of Nathaniel Wythe gent decd by **Eliz^a Wythe** one of the Exors therein named and thereupon **Miles Cary jun^r** being sworn made Oath the he wrote the said Writing at the Request of the Testator as his last Will and Testament and that he read it to him the Testor and that he approved and allowed thereof and was willing and ready to publish the same but before it could be sealed in order for the Testor to sign & publish it his Distemper increasing he suddenly lost his senses and continued so til he died about an Hour afterwards But that he the Testor was in his perfect Sense & Memory at the Time of his reading the said writing to him and his allowing thereof as his Will & **Mary Wythe** being first sworn deposeth that she was in the Room at the time of the Testor's making his said Will and heard the other depon^t **Miles Cary** read the forme to him and _ if it was his Will he the Testor answered it was absolutely his Will that he was then in his perfect sense & Memory that the depn^t went out of the room to fetch a wafer to seal the said will but when she returned she found the testor insensible & uncapable of Executing his said will & continued so til he died which was about an hour afterwards.

Whereupon the Court are of Opinion that the said Writing doth contain the true last Will & Testament of the Testor and the same being made Oath to according to Law by the said **Eliz^a Wythe** one of the Exors thereto is Ordered to be Recorded.   Teste Miles Cary C_ Cur_

   [reverse:]   **Nathl Wythe's** Will   17   R _

[1752 will of Mary Wills:]   In the name of God Amen. I Mary Wills wife of **Thomas Wills jun^r** of Warwick County and Parish Gentⁿ being in perfect Health,

15

sound Sense & Understanding, Do make and ordain this my last Will and Testament (as am impowered to do by an instrument of Writing or marriage Settlement or Contract dated March the tenth one thousand seven hundred and thirty eight from my husband Mr. Thos Wills jun^r to me) in Manner and Form following, that is to say, first and principally I recommend my Soul to Almighty God and my Body to be decently interred at the Discretion of my Execors hereafter namd. I give and bequeath unto my loving Husband Thos Wills five pounds current money. Item I give to my loving Daughter **Susannah Cole** my four Wheel chaise, Harness, and two of my _ Horses to her and her Heirs for ever. Item It is my Will and Desire that my loving Daughter **Martha Leigh** have the Use of my Gold-Watch and Chain during her natural Life, and at her Death if she leaves a Daughter then living. I give and bequeath the said Watch and Chain to that Daughter and her Heirs for ever: but if the said it shou'd so happen that my Daughter **Martha Leigh** leave no daughter as aforesaid, then it is my Will   and Desire, that the said Gold-Watch and Chain return to my loving Daughter **Jane Claiborne**, which I give unto her and her Heirs for ever. Item I give and bequeath unto my loving Daughter **Jane Claiborne** four Pounds Cash to buy her a mour[n]ing Ring. Item I give and bequeath unto my loving Daughter **Susannah Cole** one negro girl nam'd Priscilla with her Increase to her and her Heirs for ever. I likewise give unto my said Daughter Susannah Cole the Residue of the sixty two pounds ten Shillings (which was left to me by my Mother Mme [?] **Mary Blair** in her will) after the two Legacies above (to wit) the one five Pounds and the other four Pounds are paid, being fifty three Pounds ten Shilllings to her and her Heirs for ever. Item It is my Will and Desire that my old coachman Will may choose which of my Children he had rather live with and after he hath made such Choice I give the said Negro Will to him or her and their Heirs for ever. Item My Will and Desire farther is that my Daughter Susannah Cole may have all my wearing clothes after my Death. Lastly I do hereby constitute and appoint my loving Son **Roscow Cole** and my loving Daughter **Susannah Cole** Execor and Execrix of this my last Will and Testament, revoking all former Wills by me theretofore made, ratifying and confirming this to be my last Will and Testament. In Testimony whereof I have hereunto set my Hand and Seal this thirteenth Day of April, one thousand seven hundred and fifty one.   **Mary Wills [sr]**   [seal]

Signed seal'd published and declar'd to be the last Will & Testament of the Testatrix in Presence of **Eliz.^{h} Cary Martha Cary Thos Cary**. At a court held for Warwick County March 5th 1752 This Will was prov'd in court by **Roscow Cole** one of the Exors therein nam'd, who made Oath thereunto, according to Law, and the same being prov'd by the Oaths of **Thos Cary** and **Martha Cary** two of the Witnesses thereto is order'd to be recorded. And on the Motion of the said Execor Certificate if granted him for obtaining a Probat thereof in Due Form etc.   A Copy. Teste **Richd Cary** CC   [at bottom an apparently unrelated notation, probably on reused paper:] _ **Mary B_ Wills** for Mr. **Wm Claiborne**

[1760 will of Thomas Wills:]   I **Thomas Wills** of the Parish and County of Warwick being sick and weak of body but of sound & perfect Mind & Memory Thanks be to God do make and ordain this my last Will & Testament in Manner and Form following, that 1]   is to say Imprimis I recommend my Soul to God & my body to the Earth to be decently [buried] at the Discretion of my Exec hereafter named Item   I give & devise to my Daughter **Anne Wills** my   Negro Woman Fanny & her child Betty to her & her Heirs   Item   2] I give & devise to my Son **John Wills** my Negro Man Jammey (a shoe maker) and after the Death of my Wife my Negroes Mulatto Billy, Nanny & her Children, Dick, Frank & Pate to him and his Heirs   Item I give & bequeath to my Daughter **Elizabeth Wills** my Negro Woman Mirbillo & her Children Roger and Phillis to her & her Heirs and after the Death of my Wife my Negro Man great George and my Negroe Boy little Billy to her & her Heirs   Item I give & devise to my Daughter **Mary Wills** when she comes to age or marries my Negro girl Nanny and after the Death of my Wife my Negroe Man little George & my Body little Jamey to her & her Heirs   Item In case either my said Daughters Elizabeth or Mary dies without Heirs of her Body begotten living at Time of her Death then it is my Will that the Negroes before given to them be 3]   equally divided between my Son John Wills & the Survivors of my said Daughters Elizabeth or Mary   Item I give & devise to my Wife Elizabeth my Negro Woman Betty & my Negro Girl Hanah to her & her Heirs   Item I give & devise to my Wife Eliz[a] Wills (or in [4]   case of her Death before my Daughter Dorothy) to my Son **John Wills** my Negroes Pompey and Moll to & for the uses & Purposes following & for no other, to wit, for the use of my daughter Dorothy Wills during her natural life and after her Death to and for the use of my Daughter Anne Wills and her Heirs; and further 'tis my Will that my Wife have the care of my Daughter **Dorothy Person**'s & Estate and in case she survives my Wife then I will that my Son John have the care of my said Daughter's Person and Estate   Item I give& devise the use pf all the rest of my Estate real and personal & the Negroes before mentioned which are not to rest in the Legatees till after my Wife's Death which beloved **Eliz[a] Wills** during her natural life And it is my will & Desire that she be not called into an account for the Profits thereof and after my Wife's Death I desire that the personal Estate be sold and the Money arising from such Sale be equally divided between my four children **John Anne   Elizabeth [jr] & Mary Wills**   Item I give and devise to my Daughter **Mary Wills** my Negro Girl Sarah (after the Death of my Death) to her & her Heirs   Item I give & devise all my Lands to my Son **John Wills** (after the Death of my Wife) to him & his Heirs forever   Lastly I appoint my Wife **Eliz[a] Wills [Sr.]** [and my] Son John my Executrix & Executor of this my last Will & Testament hereby revoking all former Wills heretofore by me made   In Witness whereof I have hereto set my Hand & Seal this 20th Day of Dec[r] 1760   **Tho[s] Wills**   [seal]
   Signed Sealed published In presence of Rich[d] Cary Rob[-] Cary
Proved Aug[-] 10th 1766   A Copy   Rich[d] Cary C.

[1765-66 Estate Account of John Wills Jr., on the estate of William Haynes
          and petition of Richard Baker v John Wills:]   Mr John Wills Junr to the
Estate of **William Hayne**s Decd D$^-$ 1765 Decr 2

To Your Board 6 months	£6. 0.0
July } To cask lent you	2.6
To Do [ditto]	2.3
To Your Levy & poll tax	10.0
To your levy & poll tax in Southampton	1. 2.0
	7.16.9

1765 Aug 1766 May } By cask at sundry times	7.6
By ditto of **Benj^a Wills**	3. 0.0
	3. 7.6
Ball due	£ 4. 9.3
Thos. _	3___
	1. 9.3

Richard Baker one of the extors _ of Mr Haynes _ made oath before me that he
found the above acc^t so stated on the books of this Testator and that he had rec^d no
satisfaction for the same   Given under my hand this 15th February 1770 Rich^d
Hardy   To the worshipful Court of Warwick County the petition of Richd Baker
acting Exor of **William Haynes** dec^d sheweth that John Wills jun^r stands indebted to
him the sum of £4.9.3 due by acc^t and refuseth payment wherefore your petitioner
prays jud$^-$ag^t for the same with costs &c.   [reverse:] Haynes Exor v
Wills } acct.
[Some additional writing, probably in pencil, is very faint but appears to say … found
at Warwick Courthouse…

[1769 summons Hobday v Noblin (a printed fill-in-the-blanks document); the
printed words are of normal face, the filled-in words are **boldface**.]
    George the Third, by the Grace of God of Great Britain, France, and Ireland,
King, Defender of the Faith, &c. To the Sheriff of **Warwick** County, Greeting: We
command you that you summon **Matthew Noblin** to appear before our Justices of
our said County Court, at the Court-House of the said County on the **second
Thursday** in next Month then and there to answer the petition of **Wm Hobday Com
[?] w^h the Will annexed of Richd Hobson dec^d** exhibited against **him for £3. Due by
Acct** and have then there this Writ. Witness **Richd Cary** Clerk of our said Court, at
the Court-House, the 10th Day of July 1769 in the ninth Year of our Reign.   **Rich^d
Cary**
        [on reverse] copy left   **Thos Mallicote**   D Shff   [in middle
panel:] Hobday vs Noblin } Pet. Of Sum^s

18

[1773 Servant Jones' will:]   In the Name of God Amen I Servant Jones of the Parish & County of Warwick gent^n being sick & weak of body but of perfect Mind and Memory knowing all Men must die Do commit my Soul to the Almighty God in shure & certain Hope of everlasting Life through the meritorious Suffering of my Blessed Saviour Jesus Christ my body to be decently buried at the Discretion of my Executors hereafter named and so hereby authorize them to execute this my last Will and Testament revoking all others made by me whatsoever   Item I give and devise unto my Son **Allen Jones** the Land I now live on to him and his Heirs forever likewise I give my said Son Allen my grey Mare to him and his Heirs   Item my Will and Desire is that all my Slaves and their Increase with the Stocks and other Personal Estate to be sold at publick Sale at twelve Months Creditt the Purchasers giving Bond and approved Security to my s^d Executor and the Money arising therefrom to be equally divided amongst my six children **Matthew, Mary, William, James Servant, John** and my Grand Daughter **Francis Servant** (Daughter of my deceased Son **Phillip Jones**) and Case my Grand Daughter under age or without lawful Issue then her Part to be equally divided between my two Sons James Servant and John   Item   by my deceased Fathers last Will and Testament the_ Reversion of several Tracts or Parcell of Lands will be my Property at the Death of my Brother **Albridgton Jones** and when that shall happen my Will and desire is that my Exor shall bring Suit against the Person and all Persons that shall have Possession or Claim the said Lands and if the said Lands shall be recovered or any Part thereof that then my Will is that the Lands so recovered shall be sold to the highest Bidder at twelve Months Creditt the Purchasers to give Bond and approved Security to my Exor and the Money therefrom arising to be equally divided amongst my Children Allen, Matthew Mary Albridgton, William, James, John and Grand Daughter Francis Servant   Item I do hereby appoint my Son Allen Guardian to my son John to educate and bring him up as he shall think proper. I do hereby appoint my Son Allen Jones and **Robert** Error! Bookmark not defined. **Lucas** Exors of this my last Will & Testament bareing date the 20th Day November 1772   Servant Jones [seal] Signed Sealed and published in presence of **Francis Lee Cuthbert Hubbard**
     [reverse:] At a court held for Warwick County Feby 11th 1773 This Will was presented in Court by the Exors therein maned who made Oath thereto according to Law and the same being proved by the Oaths of the Witnesses thereto is ordered to be recorded and on the Motion of the said Exors who entered into £ Bond with **William Wills** and **John Dowsing** their Securities in the Penalty of £2000 & Certificate is granted them for obtaining a Probat thereof in due Form   a Copy Teste   **Richd Cary** C.Cu_

[1773 will of Elizabeth Wills:]   [This will was apparently rewritten; both versions (a & b)I havemill need an early versiojni are shown.] [a]   In the name of God Amen. I **Elizth Wills** do make this my last Will &c. the Testatrix thus gives away several specific [items] then writes as follows. Item. I desire my Cropt of all kinds made this year to be sold & the Money arising I give to be divided between two daughters Eliz[th] Wills & **Mary Wheadon** & my grandson **John Wills**. In Witness hereof I have set my hand & Seal this 1st Oct[r] 1773   Eliz[th] Wills   [seal]

At a Court held for Warwick County Jany 13th 1774 this Will proved in Court according to Law &c. A Copy   Teste Miles Cary D. C. Cur   [reverse:] Copy Let_ of the _ Eliz[a] Wills decd

[b] In the name of God Amen. I Elizabeth Wills Widow & Relict of **Thomas Wills** deceased of the Parish and County of Warwick being sick of Body but of sound Mind & Memory do make this my last Will and Testament. Imprimis I recommend my Soul to God my Maker as to my worldly Estate I dispose of in this Manner. First I direct all my just Debts be fully paid & satisfied Item I give unto my Daughter **Elizabeth Wills** one Negro Woman Hannah & her child Pate & one Bed & Furniture to her & her Heirs. Item I give unto my Daughter **Mary Wheadon** my Negro Woman Betty to her & her heirs. Item,   I give unto my Grandson **John Wills** my Negro Boy Tom _child of Betty ... his Heirs &... Item What Estate may fall to me by the Will of Brother **Nathaniel Cary** at the Death of Mrs. **Elizabeth Taylor** I give to my three Grandsons **John Wills, Tho[s] Wills** & **William** Error! Bookmark not defined.**Sheldon Wills** & their Heirs equally to be divided between them or the Survivors of them when such shall so fall Item I desire my crop[t] of all Kinds made this year may be sold & the Money arising I give to be equally divided between my two Daughters Eliz. Wills & Mary Wheadon & my Grandson John Wills Item all the rest of my Personal Estate of What Kind soever after the Payments of my just Debts I give to my Daughter Mary Wheadon to her and her Heirs Lastly I appoint my Loving Friend and Kindsman [kinsman] Benjamin Wills & my Son in Law John J. Wheadon Executors of this my last Will and Testament hereby revoking all other Wills heretofore by me made In Witness whereof I have hereunto set my Hand & Seal This Twenty first Day of October Anno Dom 1773   Signed Sealed Published & declared }

  By the Testatrix as & for her last }   Eliz Wills [seal]
  Will in presence of us   }
 Rich[d] Cary   **Nancy Allen   Martha Glanville**

The following articles are in my Possession which belong to the Estate of my dec[d] Husband Tho[s] Wills one walnut Dish a doz of leather Chairs & five _ 1 chest & Case with _ 1 pine table, 1 copper kettle 3 iron potts   2 Doz Pewter Plates Flat and I Box Iron & Heaters 1 water Jug 3 Butter Potts & 2 large Fat Pots 1 large 3 Gallon Jug 1 Gallon & 1 large chest up stairs 1 Stove Dish & six Plates _ 1 silver watch & some old Lumber Eliz Wills

 Teste Rich[d] Cary **Henry Allen**

[1780 Complaint of William & Anne Bland excerpting the will of William Harwood:]
To the worshipful Justices of Lo_ sitting in Chancery Humbly Complaining shew to

20

you Worships Your Orator and Oratrix **William Bland** and **Anne** his wife, which said Anne is the daughter and Devisee under the last Will and Testament of **William Harwood** late of the County of Warwick deceased. That the said William Harwood the father, being seized and possessed of a considerable Real, and Personal Estate, duly made his last Will and Testament in Writing bearing date the thirteenth day of _ [blank] in the year 1780. And thereby gave to your Oratrix, as followeth "I give all my Land in Stanley Hundred in the County of Warwick as follows, one fourth part to my Son **Edward**, and the other three fourths to be equally divided between my Daughters, Mary, **Margaret**, and **Anne** and my Grand Daughter **Dorothy Harwood Hewitt**, to them and Their Heirs forever. * [The following sentence might have been inserted here, but it appears on a separate sheet of paper:] I give all my Slaves, that I have not mentioned to be equally divided between my Daughter **Mary**, my Daughter **Margaret** my Daughter **Anne**, my Daughter **Dorothy** and my Grand Daughter **Dorothy Harwood Hewitt** to them and their Heirs forever." The other half of the Slaves _ my wife, not mentioned, I give to be equally divided between my Daughter Mary, my Daughter Anne, my Daughter Dorothy, and my Grand Daughter Dorothy H. Hewitt and my Grandson **William Whitaker**, and my Grandson **Richard H. Hewitt**, to them and their Heirs forever. And the Silver Spoon and her_ Estate I lent my wife during her life, I give to be equally divided between my Daughter Mary, my Daughter Martha … Margaret, my Daughter Anne, and my Grand Daughter **Dorothy Harwood Hewitt**, to them and their Heirs forever. I give all my Tobacco to be equally divided between my Daughters Mary, Margaret, Anne, Dorothy and my Grand Daughter Dorothy H. Hewitt and their Heirs. After all my Debts are fully satisfied and paid, I give the rest of my Estate, that is not given away to be equally divided between my Son Edward my Daughters Mary, Martha, Margaret, Anne, Dorothy, my Grandson **Richard H. Whitaker** to them and their Heirs, and of his said Will did nominate and appoint his son Edward, his wife Mary, **Richard Cary** and **Robert Lucas** his Executors" And your Orator and Oratrix [say] further then to your Worships that the said William Harwood your Oratrix's Father departed this life on or about the [blank] day of [blank] in the year 17 [blank] without altering or rewriting the said Will, and upon his death the said Edward one of his Executors proved the Same in the County Court of Warwick [as] will fully appear by a Certificate granted thereof on the eighth day of March in the year 1781. The other Executor in the Will named having refused to act under the Will aforesaid. That the said Edward by virtue of such Will and probate possessed himself of all the personal Estate of the said William to a very considerable amount including a very considerable amount of Tobacco, one fifth part of which was devised to your Oratrix by the Will of her Father. And your Orator, and Oratrix further shew to your Worships, that in or about the month of [blank] last past, your Orator and Oratrix Intermarried, whereby your Orator, in Right of your Oratrix his Wife, is become entitled to the Legacies so as aforesaid devised to the said Anne his wife, and your Orator and Oratrix have since their Intermarriage often applied to the said Edward

in a decent manner, and desired him to give an account of the Quantity of Tobacco, so as aforesaid left by the Testator, and to allot to your Orator his part of the Land in Stanley Hundred, and also to give an account of the __ [lined out]
Personal Estate of the Testator, and of what the same consisted, and to know how and in what manner the Personal Estate has been applied, and how much thereof remains in his Hands, and that he might pay to your Orator, and Oratrix, what shall appear justly due to them, under the said Will, and __ their part of the Slaves and your Orator well hoped that the said Edward would have complied with such reasonable Requests as in justice and equity he ought. But now so it is may it please Your Worships, that the said Executor, combining and confederating with other persons at present unknown to your Orator, whose names when discovered your Orator prays may be made Defendants to this … contriving to defeat your Orator and Oratrix of the benefit intended by the Devises intended in the said Will, refuses to give, or under any account of his administration of the said Estate, sometimes pretending that the Personal Estate of his said Testator was very small, and inconsiderable, and not sufficient to pay the Debts, Legacies, and funeral Expences . Whereas your Orator, and Oratrix charge and so the truth is, that the said Testator died possessed of a very considerable Personal Estate, much more than sufficient to pay all his just Debts, Legacies, and funeral Expences, with a great overplus. All which actings and doings are contrary to Equity and good Conscience, and tend greatly to injure and distress your Orator. In tender Consideration whereof and for as much as Matters of this Nature are properly areguable [?] in a Court of Equity. To the end therefore that the perfect answer make to all and singular the premises, as fully and particularly, and the same, were here again repeated and interrogated [?], more especially, that he may set forth and declare, whether the said **William . Harwood** did not make such last Will as herein before is set forth? Or any other, and what Will? Whether the said William did not Depart this Life, on or about the [blank] day of [blank] in the Year 17_ [blank] with out altering or revoking such Will? Whether the said Testator did not die seized, and possessed of a considerable Real and Personal Estate, in the Counties of Warwick, and Mecklenburg? Whether an Inventory and appraisement of his Personal Estate was made and returned to Court? Whether the said Executor did not alone prove the Same in the County Court of Warwick? Whether the Testator did not leave a very considerable Sum in paper Money, and whether the same came to the Hands of the Executor, and how and in what Manner has the same been disposed of? What Quantity of Tobacco left by the said Testator, came to the Hands of the said Executor? Whether the said Executor by virtue of the power vested in him by the said Will, and by the probate thereof, did not possess himself of all the Personal Estate? Whether your Orator since his Intermarriage hath not frequently applied to the said Executor to have an account of the Personal Estate of the Testator, and to be paid what should appear justly due, and owing to [h]er … [damaged] may be compelled to come to a fair _. Your O[rator] and Oratrix _ the Personal Estate [of] the said Testator, that he may be

compelled to pay to your Orator and Ora[trix] what may appear fully due to them, and that your O[rator] and Oratrix may have such for their relief in the pres_ as is consistent with Equity and good Conscience.

P[r]ay _ please __ I Prent_

[reverse:] ... vs Harwoods Ex^r } Bill   1780

Feby .... Bill _

March ......[...] ....

July .... Rep^d

Aug .... Court

Sept... Court

Octo .... Court

...

[1781, Will of Robert Lucas:] In the Name of God Amen I Robert Lucas do ...[no words following]   Item I give unto my Son **Tom Lucas** Part of my Tract of Land including the Dwelling House, out Houses orchard _ where I now live bounded by the Bottom between this _ where Burt lived thence from the Head of said Bottom to the large Hiccory [sic] by the Road thence along the said road to the Head of the Simmontree Bottom thence down said Bottom to the Mill Pond then down the Mill Pond to Mr. **Dowsing**'s line thence along the said Line to Skif's Creek I likewise give him 25 Acres in the Briery Branch joinging [sic] **General Nelson**'s to be laid off by a due North Line I likewise give him Shpney [sp?] & Venus, 10 Head Cattle, 10 Head Sheep 10 Head of Hogs 1 Bed & Furniture & 1 Sg^l [?] Folding Table The rest of my Land I desire may be sold for Tob^o or what my Executor shall think best and the produce of the said Sale to be equally divided amongst my three Sons or the Survivors of them Viz^t **Robert Gervase & John Jones Lucas** And I give my Slaves Stock and all my personal Estate to be sold & the Proceeds be equally divided amongst my children **Sally Nancey Robert Gervase Lucy Elizth** and John or the Survivors of them for their Support & Maintainance [sic] at the Discression [sic] of Guardians I appoint [my friend] Doct^r [?] Galt Guardian to my three Boys their to bring them up as He thinks [proper?] on their Estates and my Friend Mr. [?] **Trebell** Guardian of my Dau[gh]ters with the like Limitations I constitute & appoint _d Friend Col^o **Edward Harwood** ... Doct^r [?] **Galt** my Exor[s] of this my last Will and Testament this 20th Day May 1781 [?] ...   [Lu]cas   seal

Witness   Provd in Warwick County Court ... March

[?] 1782 [?]   a copy Rich^d C_

[1782 Estate account of Scervant Jones] D⁻The sale of Estate of the late Captain Servient Jones in acco^t proper with the legatees & ...

To **Wm Reynolds** his acc^t ag^t said Estate   £   13.6

To the hon^{ble} Brig^{der} **Gen Nelson** for so much as **Wm Mitchell** bought of said Estate on his acct   £   17.15.6

23

To **Wm Stevenson** for 2 hhds of Tob° paid him Ro. Lucas out of the Estate in Part of his acc^t £ 16. 4.4

To A. Js on G. W. for a Negro _ of inst sold to George30.......

To **Allen Jones**'s acct. proved   320.13.2

To **Robert Lucas**, sundries paid by him   1.16.7½

    £387. 3.1½

To ball^e due the Estate   319. 5.6

    £706. 8.9½

C^r 1782 July

By amount Sales of the Estate   703.11.9½

By an account on his Book ag^t a certain **Wm Reynolds**   13.6

    704. 5.3½

By acc^t on the Book A. Jones   2. 3.4

    706. 8.7½

By Bal^{ce} per contra   319. 5.6

By sundries sold by Allen Jones   142. 12.5½

    461.17.11½

In pursuance of an order of Warwick Court dated July 11th 1782 We the subscribers have examined the hereto Account of the Estate of Capt **Servant Jones** dec^d and we find the balance due to the said

Estate Four hundred and sixty one Pounds seventeen shillings & 11½

Current money out of which sum it appears to us that Mr **Allen Jones** is to pay eighty one pounds ten shillings & three pence the Estate of Mr **Robert Lucas** to account for three hundred and eighty pounds seven shillings & 8½ Given under hands this 12th July 1782.

Wm Cary

L_ Smith

Wm Reynolds

Nath.^{ll} **[?] Wills**

Returned into Warwick County August 8th 1782 and ordered to be recorded. a Copy

Teste **Rich**^d **Cary** C C

Index of Names

For simplification, page numbers are limited (especially where documents extend over multiple pages), therefore researchers might search adjacent pages for names sought. The spelling of names is fragile; imagination is useful.

J

James
Isabella, 3
Janes
Francis, 3
Jardin
Christanna, 4
Jenkins
Thomas, 1
Jones
Agatha, 9
Albridgton, 9, 19
Albridgton [jr], 19
Allen, 19, 24
Elizabeth, 9
Elizabeth [jr], 9
Elizabeth [sr], 9
Francis Servant, 19
James Servant, 19
Martha, 9
Mary, 19
Matthew, 3
Matthew [jr], 19
Phillip, 19
Servant, 2, 19, 24
William, 19

L

Lee
Francis, 19
Lenton
Jno, 3
Lisny
Ralph, 6
Loftis
Edward, 3
Loftys
Edward, 6
Lucas
Elizth, 23

Gervase, 23
John, 2, 9, 10
John Jones, 23
Lucy, 23
Nancey, 23
Robert, 19, 21, 23
Robert [sr], 23
Sally, 23
Tom, 23

M

Mackintosh
Enos, 10
Mallicote
Mary, 12
Thomas, 12
Thomas [jr], 12
Thos, 18
Merry, 4
Mitchell
Wm, 23
Moore, 5
Martha, 4, 5
R, 4
Richd, 3
Muschamp
Mary, 2

N

Nath
Hoggard, 10
Naylor
Elizabeth 8
Joshua 6
Nelson
Gen, 23
Noble
Jno, 2
Noblin

27

Matthew, 18

P
Padin
James, 14
Pawly
James, 3
Peare
Dorothy, 13
Person
Dorothy, 17
Philipson
Robert, 9
Phipps
Thomas, 2
Pierce
Jeremiah, 2

R
Ransha
Samll, 2, 4
Reynolds
Wm, 23
Robinson
George, 2, 3
Rodin
James, 14
Roscow
James, 13
William, 13

S
Selden
Samuel, 10
Simmons
Samll, 1
Smith
L_, 24

Stevenson
Wm, 23
Stow
John, 4
Stuckey
Anne, 10

T
Taylor
Elizabeth 20
Thompson
jun, 1
Tingnall
John, 4
Todd
Thomas, 15
Trebell, 23

W
Wheadon
Mary, 20
Whitaker
Capt, 2
Henry, 3
John, 11, 12
Richard, 4
Richard H., 21
William, 21
Whiting
Beverley, 15
Will
Emanll, 2
Wills
Anne 17
Benja, 18
Benjamin, 20
Elizabeth, 17, 20
Emanuel, 2, 5
John, 2, 9, 17, 20

28

Mary, 15, 17
Mary B, 16
Thomas, 15, 17, 20
Thomas junr, 15
William Sheldon, 20
Wilson
mr, 5
Wood
Mathew, 3
Wythe
Eliza, 15

Mary, 15
Nathaniel, 15

Y
Young
William 8
Yorgan
Andrew, 1

www.ingramcontent.com/pod-product-compliance
Lightning Source LLC
LaVergne TN
LVHW051713080426
835511LV00017B/2895